THE TOP SECRET LIFE OF PLANTS

HOW INVASIVE SPECIES TAKE OVER

BY JANEY LEVY

Gareth Stevens
PUBLISHING

Please visit our website, www.garethstevens.com. For a free color catalog of all our high-quality books, call toll free 1-800-542-2595 or fax 1-877-542-2596.

Library of Congress Cataloging-in-Publication Data

Names: Levy, Janey, author.
Title: How invasive species take over / Janey Levy.
Description: New York : Gareth Stevens Publishing, 2020. | Series: The top secret life of plants | Includes index.
Identifiers: LCCN 2018024933| ISBN 9781538233771 (library bound) | ISBN 9781538233757 (pbk.) | ISBN 9781538233764 (6 pack)
Subjects: LCSH: Invasive plants–Juvenile literature.
Classification: LCC SB613.5 .L48 2020 | DDC 581.6/2–dc23
LC record available at https://lccn.loc.gov/2018024933

First Edition

Published in 2020 by
Gareth Stevens Publishing
111 East 14th Street, Suite 349
New York, NY 10003

Copyright © 2020 Gareth Stevens Publishing

Designer: Sarah Liddell
Editor: Abby Badach Doyle

Photo credits: Cover, p. 1 (main flower) dabjola/Shutterstock.com; cover, p. 1 (background flowers) Bob C/Shutterstock.com; glass dome shape used throughout bombybamby/Shutterstock.com; leaves used throughout janniwet/Shutterstock.com; background texture used throughout MInerva Studio/Shutterstock.com; p. 5 ArjaKo's/Shutterstock.com; p. 7 (tomato plant) Ardely/Shutterstock.com; p. 7 (epiphytes) Tine Snels/Shutterstock.com; p. 9 Perfect Lazybones/Shutterstock.com; p. 11 Alvesgaspar/Wikimedia Commons; p. 13 Tareq Saifur Rahman/Moment/Getty Images; pp. 15, 17 (map) ekler/Shutterstock.com; p. 15 (Japanese honeysuckle) EuricoZimbres/Tau'olunga/Wikimedia Commons; p. 17 Mokkie/Wikimedia Commons; p. 19 Aleoks/Shutterstock.com; p. 21 Singkham/Shutterstock.com.

Printed in the United States of America

CPSIA compliance information: Batch #CS19GS: For further information contact Gareth Stevens, New York, New York at 1-800-542-2595.

CONTENTS

Words in the glossary appear in **bold** type
the first time they are used in the text.

DANGER!
INVASIVE SPECIES!

Perhaps you've heard people talk about invasive plant **species** and the dangers they present. But do you know what an invasive species is? It's one that's not native to an area. It has entered from somewhere else. And it becomes invasive when it grows well and spreads quickly in its new **habitat,** causing harm to native plants or to people who live there.

How are invasive plant species able to sneak in and cause trouble? Let's take a look at the top secret life of invasive species to discover how they take over!

CLASSIFIED!

THE TERM "INVASIVE SPECIES" USUALLY APPLIES TO PLANTS FROM ANOTHER COUNTRY. BUT IT CAN ALSO APPLY TO PLANTS THAT MOVE TO A DIFFERENT PART OF THE SAME COUNTRY.

PURPLE LOOSESTRIFE MAY BE BEAUTIFUL TO LOOK AT, BUT IT'S AN INVASIVE PLANT SPECIES THAT'S CAUSED LOTS OF HARM.

FIRST, THE BASICS

Before we talk about how invasive species take over, we must know the secrets of how *all* plants live and grow. All plants need certain things. They need light, water, **nutrients**, air, and warmth to grow.

Most plants grow from a seed. They have roots that grow down into the soil to get water and nutrients. Their stem carries water and nutrients to other plant parts. Their leaves make food through **photosynthesis** (foh-toh-SIHN-thuh-suhs) using water, nutrients, sunlight, and carbon dioxide from the air.

CLASSIFIED!

SOME PLANTS DON'T NEED SOIL BUT GROW HIGH UP ON TREES OR EVEN ON TELEPHONE POLES. THEY'RE CALLED AIR PLANTS, OR EPIPHYTES (*EHP*-UH-FYTS).

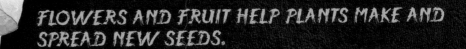

FLOWERS AND FRUIT HELP PLANTS MAKE AND
SPREAD NEW SEEDS.

PARTS OF A TOMATO PLANT

FLOWER

FRUIT

STEM

LEAF

ROOTS

epiphytes

7

HOW PLANTS TRAVEL TO NEW HABITATS

Plants aren't like animals. They can't walk, run, swim, or fly to a new place. So what are their travel secrets? How do they get to a new habitat and become an invasive species?

Seeds and weeds may sneak in within soil and plants imported, or brought in, by businesses that sell plants. Ships from other countries may have plants in the **ballast water** they let out when they dock. Sometimes plants are imported on purpose because they're beautiful or unusual.

CLASSIFIED!

PEOPLE WHO TRAVEL CAN CARRY SEEDS FROM PLACE TO PLACE ON THEIR CLOTHING OR IN THEIR SUITCASE.

SEEDS CAN EVEN HIDE ON THE OUTSIDE OF PLANES THAT TRAVEL BETWEEN COUNTRIES.

LIFE IN A NEW PLACE
MAY FAIL

Just because a plant reaches a new habitat doesn't mean it will become invasive. First, conditions must be right. If a seed for a plant that grows in a hot, dry place lands in a cool, wet place, the plant won't be able to grow.

If conditions are right, the nonnative plant must be able to **compete** with native plants for **resources**. It may compete well enough to survive, but not to become invasive. But if it can't compete, it will die.

THIS WILDFLOWER IS A NONNATIVE PLANT IN ENGLAND THAT HASN'T BECOME INVASIVE.

11

THE SECRETS TO SUCCESS

Nonnative plants that become invasive share certain secrets to success. They're strong growers that produce a lot of seeds. They're able to **adapt** well to many different conditions. They have an advantage because they're away from the bugs, sicknesses, and predators that limited them in their original habitat. And these limiting elements don't exist for them in their new habitat.

Some invasive plants have even sneakier secrets. Their leaves or roots put out poisons that slow the growth of other plants!

CLASSIFIED!

WATER HYACINTH IS NATIVE TO THE AMAZON RIVER IN SOUTH AMERICA. IT WAS IMPORTED INTO THE UNITED STATES IN 1884, INTO AFRICA IN 1892, AND INTO ASIA IN 1894.

WATER HYACINTH IS A BEAUTIFUL BUT INVASI
PLANT THAT HAS CHOKED WATERWAYS AROU
THE WORLD.

PURPLE LOOSESTRIFE AND JAPANESE HONEYSUCKLE

The United States has many invasive plant species. But some have been more wildly successful—and harmful—than others. One of the most common has been purple loosestrife. It was imported in the early 1800s for use as decoration and to make medicine. It's now invasive in most states.

Japanese honeysuckle was brought to Long Island, New York, in 1806 for use as decoration and to help control erosion. It's now invasive along much of the East Coast.

CLASSIFIED!

A SINGLE PURPLE LOOSESTRIFE PLANT CAN PRODUCE 2 MILLION SEEDS PER YEAR. THE WIND HELPS SPREAD THOSE SEEDS FAR FROM THE ORIGINAL PLANT.

PURPLE LOOSESTRIFE IS SUCH A SUCCESSFUL INVASIVE PLANT THAT IT'S BEEN ABLE TO SPREAD TO ALMOST EVERY STATE, AS THIS MAP SHOWS.

PURPLE LOOSESTRIFE IN THE UNITED STATES

PURPLE LOOSESTRIFE FOUND

PURPLE LOOSESTRIFE NOT FOUND

.... Japanese honeysuckle

ENGLISH IVY
AND KUDZU

English ivy was imported before the United States even was founded as a country. Colonists brought it in the early 1700s because it was easy to grow and stayed green through winter. It's now a common invasive plant that can grow strong enough to kill trees!

Japan presented kudzu at a world's fair in Philadelphia, Pennsylvania, in 1876. The **vine** was first presented as a decorative plant, then as a food crop for farm animals. It was later planted to prevent soil erosion. It's now invasive in the Southeast.

CLASSIFIED!

KUDZU GROWS UP TO 1 FOOT (30 CM) PER DAY AND 60 FEET (18 M) PER YEAR! LIKE ENGLISH IVY, IT CAN KILL TREES.

ENGLISH IVY HAS BEEN ABLE TO SPREAD WIDELY ACROSS THE UNITED STATES, AS THIS MAP SHOWS. IT HAS EVEN REACHED ALASKA AND HAWAII!

ENGLISH IVY IN THE UNITED STATES

ENGLISH IVY FOUND

ENGLISH IVY NOT FOUND

· · · · · · · · English ivy

HARM CAUSED BY INVASIVE SPECIES

It's surprising that some invasive species can kill trees. But they can do more than that, too. They can reduce the number of kinds of plants in an area by competing more successfully for resources. That hurts the bugs, birds, and other animals that depend on those plants for habitats or food.

Invasive plants can lead to poor soil conditions for growing crops. They can reduce water quality, or grade.

CLASSIFIED!

BY CHANGING HABITATS, INVASIVE SPECIES CAN REDUCE OPPORTUNITIES FOR PEOPLE TO ENJOY OUTDOOR ACTIVITIES IN CERTAIN AREAS.

They can lead to increased soil erosion. In short, invasive species can completely change a habitat.

THE NORWAY MAPLE WAS BROUGHT TO NOR
AMERICA IN 1756. THE INVASIVE TREE CROWL
OUT NATIVE TREES AND CREATES SO MUCH SH
IT KEEPS WILDFLOWERS FROM GROWING.

1

WHAT CAN YOU DO?

By using all their secrets to success, invasive plants have become a real problem. But there are things you—and everyone—can do to help. First, find out which plants are invasive in your area. Contact your local native plant society or state Department of Natural Resources to find out. Then learn to recognize them.

Remove invasive plants around your home. When you add new outdoor plants at home, use only native or noninvasive plants. Teach family and friends about invasive plants.

EVERYONE CAN PLAY A PART IN CONTROLLING INVASIVE PLANTS.

GLOSSARY

adapt: to change to suit conditions

ballast water: the water kept in tanks on ships to help keep them steady and balanced

carbon dioxide: a gas in the air used by plants to make food

compete: to try to get something that others are also trying to get

erosion: the act of wearing away by water, wind, or ice

habitat: the natural place where an animal or plant lives

nutrient: something a living thing needs to grow and stay alive

photosynthesis: the way plants make food using sunlight

resource: a usable supply of something

species: a group of plants or animals that are all the same kind

vine: a plant that cannot stand up on its own but must grow by climbing over an object or other plants

FOR MORE INFORMATION

BOOKS

Chung, Liz. *Controlling Invasive Species*. New York, NY: PowerKids Press, 2017.

Pearson, Scott. *Kudzu*. Mankato, MN: Black Rabbit Books, 2017.

Spilsbury, Richard. *Invasive Plant Species*. New York, NY: PowerKids Press, 2015.

WEBSITES

Go Wild with Native Gardening
www.nature.org/ourinitiatives/regions/northamerica/unitedstates/native-non-native-and-invasive-plants-what-does-a-gardener-need-to-know.xml
This site talks about the benefits of native plant species over invasive species and provides clear examples of the harm done by invasive species.

Invasive Plants
ccetompkins.org/environment/invasive-nuisance-species/invasive-plants
Learn more about some common invasive plants and find a list of invasive plants in the United States on this website.

Understanding and Controlling Invasive Plant Species
ccetompkins.org/environment/invasive-nuisance-species/invasive-plants
Learn more about some common invasive plants and find a list of invasive plants in the United States on this website.

INDEX